vegan.

KYRA DE VREEZE, naturopath

vegan.

RECIPES FOR A MORE DELICIOUS LIFE

Leabharlanna Poiblí Chathair Baile Átha Cliath
Dublin City Public Libraries

MURDOCH BOOKS
SYDNEY · LONDON

Published in 2018 by Murdoch Books, an imprint of Allen & Unwin
Published in 2017 by Kosmos Uitgevers

Murdoch Books Australia
83 Alexander Street,
Crows Nest NSW 2065
Phone: +61 (0)2 8425 0100
murdochbooks.com.au
info@murdochbooks.com.au

Murdoch Books UK
Ormond House, 26–27 Boswell Street,
London WC1N 3JZ
Phone: +44 (0) 20 8785 5995
murdochbooks.co.uk
info@murdochbooks.co.uk

For corporate orders and custom publishing contact our business development
team at salesenquiries@murdochbooks.com.au

Publisher: Corinne Roberts
English language editor: Kay Halsey
Translator: Tineke Millard
Production Director: Lou Playfair

Text and photography © Kyra de Vreeze/Kosmos Uitgevers, Utrectht/Antwerpen
Design: Rosa Kuiper Design www.rosakuiper.com

ISBN 978 1 76063 768 2 Australia
ISBN 978 1 91163 211 5 UK

A cataloguing-in-publication entry is available from the catalogue
of the National Library of Australia at nla.gov.au
A catalogue record for this book is available from the British Library

Printed by Hang Tai Printing Company, China

INTRODUCTION

I was sixteen when I decided to eat vegetarian food. If it had been up to me, I would have been a vegetarian from three years old, but eating meat was very normal in our family. When I learnt to cook, I took control. The choice was twofold for me: I didn't like the taste or texture of meat and I am somewhat of an idealist in nature. The idea that an animal had to die and I would then put it in my body, was unthinkable to me.

I did not eat cheese or egg, not even as a vegetarian, so taking the step to fully plant-based foods was easy to do. I was 26. The main reason to go vegan was that I felt at my fittest when I ate a fully plant-based diet. My irritable bowel problems were solved completely and I felt that my body was moving more supply and easily when I practised yoga.

For years I ate vegan food only, until my body indicated that it needed something extra. I now have some biological raw milk yoghurt and ghee in addition to all the plant-based food. Why this change? I listen to my body and needs and do not live dogmatically. I am of the belief that everyone would benefit from a simple, unrefined and pure diet which is primarily composed of plants. This diet is not a hype, it is our nature. Humans have always eaten like this.

Some people – to feel at their best – will need to supplement this with a small amount of animal-based food. That is a personal choice.

Cooking plant-based foods is not something a lot of us have learnt at home. It is a cooking style which gives vegetables the leading role. These vegetables, together with full grains, nuts, beans, herbs and spices, ensure a full-value meal. This cooking style requires some knowledge, but primarily a lot of practical experience. It is a matter of doing it again and again and again.

Chances are that you picked up this book because you are interested in cooking plant-based foods. Maybe you were raised as an omnivore like me and now you want to learn how to prepare a balanced vegan meal. Maybe you enjoy a piece of meat but want to eat plant-based foods during the week. Maybe you have physical complaints which require you to start eating pure and unrefined foods. Maybe you have been eating vegan for years and you are looking for new recipes. Whatever the reason, and whatever experience you may have, *vegan* will give you inspiration and practical tips on how you can cook yummy plant-based foods with ease.

The book contains breakfasts, lunches, snacks, dinners and desserts. Some recipes are ridiculously easy, others a bit more complicated. The easy ones are good for during the week, the time-consuming recipes are best for the weekend. Hence the book offers delicious options for any moment and anyone.

Have fun cooking!
XOXO Kyra

My personal favourite foods are: pineapple and basil juice, mango custard, beetroot quiche, beetroot croquettes, mulberry bonbons, pitta pizzas, Beluga lentil salad, stuffed dates, raw curry and Graceland ice cream cake. Oh, yes, and coffee-sub smoothie, Matcha cream, savoury nut crackers and millet porridge. Ooh, and the dressing for the radish and samphire salad! And how about the tamarind sauce and the cherry cobbler?

Seasons

A season is listed for each recipe. This indicates what time of year the ingredients are easy to get hold of, and when the meal is most appropriate. Melon ice cream in winter is fine, but it is more suited to warmer days. Have fun with the seasonal indication, but use it as a guideline rather than a rule.

Soaking

This is not mentioned in the recipes, but it is best to soak the beans, nuts and grains for one night before you cook or process them. Put them in a bowl with lukewarm water in the evening, cover the bowl and let them soak. Drain the water the following day, rinse the beans, nuts or grains and put them in a pan or blender. Soaking has two important benefits. Firstly the soaking process shortens the cooking time. So your food will be on the table faster. In addition, soaking has a health-promoting effect. The skin of each bean, nut or grain contains phytic acid. This substance slows down the absorption of minerals in your food. Soaking and then cooking, germinating or baking beans, nuts and grains, removes a great part of the phytic acid and makes your meal more nutritious.

Measurements

1 handful of grains or nuts	about 25 gram
1 teaspoon	about 4 gram
1 tablespoon	about 14 gram
1 pinch	amount you can hold between a thumb and index finger
1 dash	3 times as much as a pinch

Kitchen equipment

To make the recipes you will need a gas stove, refrigerator or freezer, oven and hand blender. Bench-top blender, food processor and centrifugal juicer are handy but not essential.

recipes.

breakfast.

breakfast
gluten-free
spring

BUCKWHEAT 'POFFERTJES' (MINI PANCAKES) WITH CACAO SPREAD

Ingredients

Makes 2 small serves
Time 10–15 minutes

POFFERTJES
¾ cup (100 g) buckwheat
  flour
½ red onion, finely
  chopped
10 fresh lemon balm
  leaves, finely chopped,
  or 2 pinches of grated
  lemon zest
coconut oil

SPREAD
1 Hass avocado
2 Tbsp rice syrup
2 Tbsp cacoa or carob
  powder
dash of lemon juice
pinch of sea salt
½ tsp black pepper

TO SERVE
sea salt
red onion rings
fresh lemon balm

Method

To make the poffertjes, mix the flour with ½ cup (125 ml) of water to make a pancake batter. Add the chopped red onion and lemon balm or zest. Heat a little coconut oil in a frying pan to just below smoking point. Add small amounts of batter to the pan to make the poffertjes and flip them when the bases are set (buckwheat flour pancakes will stay paler than regular pancakes).

To make the spread, blend all the ingredients in a food processor or blender to make a creamy mixture. Spread over the poffertjes. Sprinkle with a little sea salt, some onion slices and extra lemon balm leaves to serve.

ANISEED SMOOTHIE WITH CHERRIES

Ingredients

Makes 2 serves
Time 5 minutes

2 tsp aniseed
200 g (7 oz) frozen sour
  cherries, thawed*
200 g (7 oz) bananas
juice of 1 orange
1 tsp nutmeg powder

TO SERVE
fresh basil leaves, (nut)
  yoghurt and buckwheat
  groats or hemp seeds
  (optional)

Method

Soak the aniseed in ½ cup (125 ml) of hot water for
3 minutes and then strain out the aniseed.

Blend the cherries, banana, orange juice, nutmeg and
aniseed tea in a blender or food processor until creamy.
Pour the smoothie into a tall glass. Garnish with basil
and yoghurt and sprinkle some buckwheat or hemp
seeds on top.

* Sour cherries can be found in the freezer section
of your health food store.

TARRAGON AND DATE CAKE

Ingredients

Makes 1 cake
Time 1 hour plus soaking

2 Tbsp whole linseeds
⅓ cup (50 g) pepitas
  (pumpkin seeds)

DRY INGREDIENTS
1½ cups (200 g)
  buckwheat flour
⅓ cup (50 g) chestnut flour
2 tsp baking powder
pinch of sea salt
4 Tbsp chopped
  fresh tarragon (or
  2 Tbsp aniseed)

WET INGREDIENTS
3 tsp vanilla extract
1½ cups (325 ml) date
  syrup
10 dried dates, pitted
1 cup (250 ml) coconut oil

TO SERVE
(nut) yoghurt or cream,
  mandarin segments, fresh
  sage leaves and pepitas
  (pumpkin seeds)

Method

Preheat the oven to 170°C (325°F). Grind the linseeds with a mortar and pestle or coffee grinder, mix with 6 tablespoons water and leave to soak for 30–60 minutes.

Place all the dry ingredients in a large bowl and mix together well. Take a second bowl and combine the wet ingredients with the linseed mixture. Add the wet ingredients to the dry and mix everything well.

Spoon the batter into a 20 x 10 x 6 cm (8 x 4 x 2½ inch) loaf tin and sprinkle with pumpkin seeds. Bake for 40–45 minutes or until cooked through. Let it cool before you cut and serve with yoghurt or cream, mandarin segments, sage leaves and a sprinkling of pumpkin seeds.

STAR ANISE MUESLI WITH MACADAMIA 'YOGHURT'

Ingredients

Makes 4–5 serves
Time 30 minutes
  plus soaking

MUESLI
**1½ cups (150 g) rolled
  oats**
½ cup (50 g) rice flakes
2 tsp vanilla extract
**⅓ cup (50 g) macadamia
  nuts**
9 star anise, crushed
⅓ cup (100 g) rice syrup
3 Tbsp pistachio nuts
1 Tbsp fresh thyme

MACADAMIA 'YOGHURT'
**⅔ cup (100 g) macadamia
  nuts**
2 Tbsp rice syrup
2 dashes of lemon juice

TO SERVE
fresh seasonal fruit

Method

Preheat the oven to 180°C (350°F). To make the muesli, mix together the oats, rice flakes, vanilla, macadamia nuts, star anise and rice syrup. Spread evenly on a baking tray lined with baking paper and bake for 15 minutes or until light golden, turning occasionally.

Allow to cool and then add the pistachio nuts and thyme. Store the muesli in an airtight container – it will gradually absorb the star anise flavour, so will taste stronger every day.

To make the yoghurt, let the macadamia nuts soak overnight in a scant ½ cup (100–120 ml) of lukewarm water. Don't have the time? Soak them for 1 hour in boiling hot water. Drain and rinse them, then combine with the rice syrup, lemon juice and ½ cup (125 ml) of water. Blend to a creamy yoghurt with a food processor or blender. It is best to start with a little bit of water, slowly adding more and more water until the yoghurt has the right consistency. For a velvety smooth result, keep the food processor running for a long time.

Serve the yoghurt and muesli with fresh seasonal fruit such as thin slices of pear or peach.

PUMPKIN-CHIA PUDDING WITH MATCHA

Ingredients

Makes 2 serves
Time 15 minutes plus
  setting and freezing
  (optional)

CHIA LAYER
¾ cup (185 g) pumpkin
  purée*
2 Tbsp coconut cream**
juice of 2 oranges
1 Tbsp grated fresh ginger
2 pinches of cayenne
  pepper
6 drops of vanilla extract
2 tsp extra virgin olive oil
6 handfuls of chia seeds

MATCHA LAYER
6 Tbsp coconut cream**
4 Tbsp rice syrup
1 tsp matcha green tea
  powder
30 drops of vanilla extract

Method

Make the chia layer by mixing the pumpkin purée, coconut cream, orange juice, grated ginger, cayenne and vanilla in a food processor. Let the motor run while you slowly add the olive oil until you have a smooth liquid. Pour into a bowl and add the chia seeds. Stir the seeds carefully into the liquid with a spoon or spatula so that they are fully covered and do not stick together. Spoon the pudding into 2 glasses or bowls and set aside for at least an hour or overnight.

Make the matcha layer by whisking the coconut cream, rice syrup, matcha powder and vanilla in a bowl to make a beautiful creamy mixture. Pour over the pumpkin-chia layer, then leave in the freezer for 30 minutes to make firmer. Don't have the time? Skip this stage and serve the pudding immediately.

TIP For a completely raw version, use pumpkin juice, raw coconut cream, a vanilla bean and a natural liquid sweetener.

* You can buy pumpkin purée or make it yourself by baking chopped pumpkin for 30–40 minutes in a 190°C (375°F) oven and then mashing.

** I use the solid parts of a BPA-free tin of coconut milk.

breakfast
gluten-free
spring & summer

CHERRY AND CHOCOLATE PORRIDGE

Ingredients

Makes 2 serves
Time 1 hour

PORRIDGE
4 handfuls of black rice
4 dried or 2 Medjool
  dates, pitted and diced
scant ½ cup (100 ml) nut
  milk*
20 drops of vanilla extract
1 Tbsp raw cacao powder

TOPPING
frozen sour cherries,
  thawed
2 Tbsp hemp seeds
fresh sage leaves, chopped
  (optional)

Method

To make the porridge, place the rice and dates in a pan with 1¼ cups (310 ml) water. Heat so the rice is just at boiling point, then stir carefully and shortly every 15 minutes until the rice has been cooking for 45 minutes.

Add the nut milk, vanilla and cacoa powder. Stir to combine and then simmer for another 15 minutes over a low heat. Spoon into bowls and top with the cherries, hemp seeds and sage leaves.

* I use rice-almond or rice-hazelnut milk.

MILLET PORRIDGE WITH ALMOND MILK, APRICOTS AND VANILLA

Ingredients

Makes 2 serves
Time 1 hour

²/₃ cup (100 g) millet
scant 1 cup (225 ml)
  almond milk
1 vanilla bean
6 unsulphured apricots,
  cut into strips, halves
  or left whole
2 Tbsp rice syrup
1 dash of orange juice
1 tsp grated orange zest

Method

Put the millet and 2 cups (500 ml) water in a saucepan. Bring just up to the boil and cook for 30–40 minutes over very low heat, stirring carefully every 15 minutes or so, then turn off the heat. Add the almond milk and bring up to the boil again for another 15 minutes. Split and scrape the vanilla bean and add the seeds to the porridge.

Place the apricots in another pan with a little bit of water and the empty vanilla bean. Boil for 15 minutes until all the water has evaporated.

Put the millet porridge in a blender and add the rice syrup and orange juice. Keep the motor running until it is smooth and creamy. Spoon into bowls and sprinkle with the apricots and a little bit of orange zest.

TIP To save time, you can boil the millet the night before.

SPICY BREAKFAST SALAD

Ingredients

Makes 2 small serves
Time 15 minutes

DRESSING
2 tsp grated fresh ginger
2 Tbsp extra virgin olive oil
1 tsp cayenne powder
1 small roasted garlic
   clove, peeled
2 tsp rice syrup
pinch of sea salt

SALAD
1 small grapefruit
1 orange
1 blood orange
1 handful of coriander
   (cilantro) leaves
nigella seeds (optional)

Method

To make the dressing, put all the ingredients in a blender and mix until smooth.

To make the salad, cut the ends off the grapefruit, orange and blood orange, then slice off the skin and pith, working with the contours of the fruit. Cut into rounds and put in a bowl. Squeeze the juice from the leftover parts of the fruit into the bowl as well. Add the dressing and sprinkle with coriander and nigella seeds.

TIP Do you want to make this meal completely raw? Use raw garlic and a natural liquid sweetener.

lunch.

ZUCCHINI AND COCONUT SOUP WITH CORIANDER

Ingredients

Makes 2 serves
Time 15 minutes

1 tsp coconut oil
1 large pinch of cumin
  seeds
1 small white onion,
  cut into rings
300 g (10 oz) zucchini
  (courgettes), sliced
10 peppercorns
3 tsp coconut cream
2 pinches of ground
  cardamom
1 pinch of cumin powder
sea salt

TO SERVE
finely sliced red onion
fresh coriander (cilantro)
  leaves

Method

Heat the coconut oil in a deep frying pan and slowly fry the cumin seeds. Add the onion and fry until translucent. Stir in the zucchini. Add the peppercorns and 2 cups (500 ml) of water and bring to the boil. Cover and simmer for 10 minutes over low heat. Turn off the heat when the zucchini is soft.

Add the coconut cream, cardamom, ground cumin and sea salt to taste. Put everything in a blender and mix to a creamy soup.

Garnish with the finely sliced onion and fresh coriander to serve.

FENNEL AND APPLE SALAD WITH RYE

Ingredients

Makes 2 serves
Time 1 hour

SALAD
70 g (2 ½ oz) rye*
¼ cup (25 g) walnuts
1 fennel bulb
1 green apple
3 Tbsp chopped fresh dill
sea salt and black pepper

DRESSING
2 Tbsp mustard
2 Tbsp lemon juice
2 Tbsp rice syrup
2 Tbsp extra virgin olive oil

TO SERVE
lemon wedges

Method

To make the salad, place the rye in a pan, cover with 3 times the amount of water and bring it to the boil. Turn down the heat and cook the rye for about 1 hour or until soft.

Heat a dry frying pan and toast the walnuts until golden.

Cut the fennel lengthways into thin slices. Cut half the apple into thin slices. Heat a chargrill pan and grill the fennel and apple on both sides until the famous grill stripes appear. Julienne the other half of the apple into thin matchsticks.

Combine all the ingredients for the dressing in a blender with 2 tablespoons of water and mix until creamy.

Drain and cool the rye and then add the dill. Add the fennel and apple and sprinkle everything with the walnuts and dressing. Season with black pepper and sea salt and add lemon wedges to serve.

* You can replace the rye with another grain, such as wholegrain couscous, barley or spelt.

SMOKED TEMPEH AND PEAR SALAD

Ingredients

Makes 2 serves
Time 15–25 minutes

3 Tbsp maple syrup
¼ tsp turmeric powder
100 g (3½ oz) smoked
  tempeh, in thin slices
1 large pear, peeled
6 Tuscan kale leaves,
  stems removed*
2 tsp coconut oil
4 Tbsp pepitas (pumpkin
  seeds)
1 Tbsp coconut oil
1½–2 Tbsp pumpkin
  seed oil**
grated zest of 1 lemon
dash of lemon juice
sea salt and black pepper

Method

Mix together the maple syrup and turmeric. Place the tempeh slices in a bowl and sprinkle with the maple marinade. Make sure that the marinade is spread well and set aside while you prepare the rest of the salad.

Place the peeled pear in a pan of boiling water and cook for 15–20 minutes until soft. Drain and leave to cool.

Remove the stems of the Tuscan kale and cut the leaves into small strips. Heat the coconut oil in a frying pan and fry the kale for a minute or two.

Grill the pumpkin seeds in a dry frying pan until they start to pop and jump, then set aside in a bowl. Add 1 tablespoon of coconut oil to the warm frying pan and bake the marinated tempeh slices until golden on both sides.

Dice the cooked pear. Place the pear, kale and tempeh in a bowl and top with the pumpkin seeds, pumpkin seed oil, lemon zest, lemon juice, sea salt and black pepper.

* Can't find Tuscan kale? Replace it with ordinary kale.

** Pumpkin seed oil can also easily be replaced with extra virgin olive oil.

APPLE AND ASPARAGUS SALAD

Ingredients

Makes 2 mains or
  4 side dishes
Time 20 minutes

SALAD
**200 g (7 oz) green
  asparagus spears**
**200 g (7 oz) zucchini
  (courgettes), cut into
  thick ribbons**
**200 g (7 oz) apple,
  cut into ribbons**
**⅓ cup (40 g) roasted
  slivered almonds**

DRESSING
**4 Tbsp white almond
  butter**
**scant ½ cup (100 ml)
  orange, mandarin
  or lemon juice**
sea salt and black pepper

Method

To make the salad, blanch the asparagus spears in hot water for 5 minutes. Cook the zucchini and apple in a dry frying pan or chargrill pan.

Use a blender to make a creamy dressing of the almond butter, juice, sea salt and black pepper.

Drain the asparagus, add the zucchini and apple and sprinkle with the dressing. Scatter the roasted almonds over the salad to serve.

TIP If asparagus is not in season, you can use steamed Brussels sprouts or green beans.

RADISH AND SAMPHIRE SALAD

Ingredients

Makes 2–3 serves
Time 10 minutes

SALAD
**200 g (7 oz) radishes,
thinly sliced**
100 g (3½ oz) samphire
2 avocados, diced
**6 handfuls of fresh parsley,
finely chopped**
**2 handfuls of fresh mint
leaves**

DRESSING
juice of 2 grapefruit
**4 dried dates, pitted
and diced**
4 Tbsp extra virgin olive oil
sea salt and black pepper

Method

Combine all the ingredients for the salad.

Make a dressing by mixing the grapefruit juice and dates in a blender, then adding the olive oil drop by drop. Keep mixing until you have a beautiful creamy and smooth dressing.

Sprinkle the dressing over the salad. Season to taste with sea salt and some freshly ground black pepper.

RED LENTIL SOUP

Ingredients

Makes 2–3 serves
Time 30 minutes

½ cup (100 g) dried
  red lentils
1 strip of kombu seaweed
1–2 Tbsp coconut oil
2 tsp cumin seeds
2 tsp mustard seeds
1 tsp ground cardamom
1 tsp turmeric powder
1 cup (250 ml) coconut
  milk
lemon juice, to taste
sea salt and black pepper

GARNISH
1–2 Tbsp coconut oil
1 white onion, cut in rings
1 tsp sesame oil
fresh coriander (cilantro)
  leaves (optional)
nuts (optional)

Method

Place the red lentils and kombu in a pan and cover with boiling water. Cover the pan and cook for 25 minutes over low heat.

Meanwhile heat the coconut oil in a frying pan and add the cumin and mustard seeds. Turn down the heat and add the other spices when they start to smell good and pop. Mix everything well, then add the herbs and spices to the lentils. Add the coconut milk and then transfer to a blender and mix until you have a creamy soup. Season to taste with the sea salt, black pepper and lemon juice.

For the garnish, heat some more coconut oil in a frying pan and sauté the onion. Serve the soup in bowls and sprinkle with the onion rings, sesame oil and maybe some coriander or nuts.

HIJIKI SALAD WITH QUINOA AND CARROT RIBBONS

Ingredients

Makes 2–3 serves
Time 25 minutes

SALAD
**20–25 g (1 oz) dried
   hijiki seaweed
2 tsp nigella seeds
½ cup (100 g) quinoa
4 Tbsp sesame oil
8 Tbsp orange or
   lemon juice
1 large carrot, cut into
   ribbons and steamed
   for 5 minutes
1 handful of leek sprouts
   or other sprouts
1 tsp grated orange zest
sea salt and black pepper**

Method

Soak the seaweed in just boiled water for 10 minutes. Drain and cool.

Meanwhile toast the nigella seeds in a dry frying pan until they are golden.

Boil the quinoa in twice as much water over low heat for 10 minutes. Turn off the heat, cover with a lid and leave for at least another 10 minutes.

With your hands, massage the sesame oil and lemon juice into the seaweed. Drain any surplus water from the quinoa and mix together all the ingredients to serve.

BELUGA LENTIL SALAD

Ingredients

Makes 2–3 serves
Time 1 hour

8 handfuls of beluga lentils
4 Tbsp extra virgin olive oil
4 handfuls of rocket
  (arugula)
20 Kalamata olives,
  cut in rings
sea salt and black pepper

DAIKON PICKLE
140 g (5 oz) daikon/
  Japanese radish
  (or regular radishes)
1 tsp dried dill
apple cider vinegar

FENNEL-PISTACHIO PESTO
4 small garlic cloves, sliced
1 Tbsp mild olive oil
50 g (2 oz) fennel
1/3 cup (50 g) pistachio
  nuts, shelled
2 large tsp fresh thyme
  leaves, no stems
6 Tbsp extra virgin olive oil
4 pinches of sea salt
lemon juice, to taste

Method

Make the daikon pickle by cutting the daikon into fine rings and putting in a bowl with the dill and enough apple cider vinegar to cover. Let everything marinate for 1 hour.

Meanwhile, boil the lentils in water over low heat for 20 minutes until al dente. Turn off the heat, cover the pan and leave to soak for 5–10 minutes. Drain the lentils and toss with the olive oil.

To make the pesto, first fry the garlic slices in the mild olive oil until golden. Transfer to a food processor and blend with all the other pesto ingredients.

Toss the lentils with the pesto, rocket and olives.

Strain the pickled daikon and add it to the salad. Season to taste with extra sea salt and pepper.

TIP You can shorten the preparation time by making the pickle beforehand. Then the salad will be on the table in 30 minutes.

snacks.

STUFFED DATES

Ingredients

Makes 8 dates
Time 5 minutes

2 Tbsp white almond butter
50 g (2 oz) seedless cucumber, cut in small cubes
12 fresh mint leaves, cut in thin strips
1 generous dash of lemon juice
8 Medjool dates, cut lengthways and pitted
8 tufts of garden cress
1 tsp grated lemon zest
sea salt

Method

Make the stuffing by mixing the almond butter, cucumber, mint, lemon juice and sea salt. Fill the dates with the stuffing and top with a tuft of garden cress and some grated lemon zest.

MULBERRY BONBONS

Ingredients

Makes 8 bonbons
Time 1 hour plus chilling

scant ¼ cup (40 g) black
  or brown rice
3 tsp sunflower or
  almond paste
30 g (1 oz) mulberries
20 drops of vanilla extract
3 Medjool dates, pitted
1 handful of hemp seeds

Method

Cook the rice according to the packet instructions for 40 minutes until all the water has been absorbed.

Make a rough paste of the cooked rice, sunflower or almond paste, mulberries, vanilla and dates in a food processor or blender. Shape the mixture into little balls with your hands. Roll the balls through the hemp seeds until well coated in seeds. Cover and place in the fridge for 1–2 hours to firm up before serving.

TIPS Do you have leftover rice? Use it to make these bonbons instead. You will need ½ cup (100 g) of cooked rice.

The bonbons will keep for a few days if kept cool and in a closed container.

PINEAPPLE AND BASIL JUICE

Ingredients

Makes 2 serves
Time 2 minutes

2 handfuls of fresh basil
400 g (14 oz) pineapple,
thinly peeled but keep
the core

Method

Juice the basil using a centrifugal juicer or slow juicer. Cut the pineapple into pieces and juice the fruit as well as the core. Add the basil juice to the pineapple juice, stir well and serve.

GREEN MOCKTAIL

Ingredients

Makes 2 small serves
Time 3 minutes

400 g (14 oz) pear
2 sticks of celery
1 kiwi, peeled
30 g (1 oz) baby leaf
  lettuce
½ small avocado
1 Tbsp fresh thyme,
  no stems

Method

Juice the pear and celery using a centrifugal juicer or slow juicer. Mix the juice, kiwi, lettuce, avocado and thyme in a blender. Blend well and serve.

snacks
gluten-free & raw
spring & summer

FRESH FENNEL SMOOTHIE WITH MINT

Ingredients

Makes 2 large serves
Time 3 minutes

800 g (1 lb 12 oz) apples
150 g (5½ oz) fennel
200 g (7 oz) cucumber
125 g (4½ oz) banana
2 handfuls of lamb's
 lettuce
1 handful of fresh mint

Method

Use a centrifugal juicer or slow juicer to juice the apples, fennel and cucumber. Place the juice in a blender and add the other ingredients to make a creamy smoothie. You can also use a hand-held blender for this.

TIP You can prepare the smoothies beforehand and freeze them. Remove them from the freezer 20–30 minutes before serving.

snack
gluten-free & raw
spring

COFFEE-SUB SMOOTHIE

Ingredients

Makes 2 serves
Time 2 minutes

1 cup (250 ml) fresh
  grapefruit juice
scant ¼ cup (50 ml) lemon
  juice
2 small bananas
12 fresh basil leaves
4 large pinches of cayenne
  pepper

Method

Mix all the ingredients in a blender and serve.

TIP This coffee-sub smoothie is a perfect alternative to a cup of coffee. It gives you a boost, just like coffee, but has nutritional value at the same time.

SAVOURY NUT CRACKERS

Ingredients

Makes 25–30 crackers
Time 50–60 minutes

DRY INGREDIENTS
scant 1½ cups (225 g) rice
   flour
¾ cup (75 g) rice flakes
generous 1 cup (150 g)
   hazelnuts, finely minced
½ cup (75 g) pepitas
   (pumpkin seeds)
1 tsp baking powder
1–2 tsp sea salt, plus extra
   for sprinkling
3 handfuls of fresh thyme
   leaves, no stems

WET INGREDIENTS
¼ cup (75 g) rice syrup
scant ¼ cup (50 ml) mild
   olive oil

TO SERVE
homemade beetroot
   hummus, finely sliced
   radish and fennel tops

Method

Preheat the oven to 190°C (375°F).

Combine all the dry ingredients and stir. Combine all the wet ingredients in a second bowl with about ½ cup (100–150 ml) water and stir. Combine the wet and dry ingredients and mix to a moist dough. Spread on a baking tray lined with baking paper. Use a second piece of baking paper to press the dough down and shape into a rectangle.

Make horizontal and vertical lines in the dough with a knife, so that the shape of the crackers is clear and they can be separated easily. Make sure the dough is not too thick. Sprinkle with some extra sea salt.

Bake in the oven for 40 minutes until golden, then let the crackers cool on a wire rack.

The crackers will keep for several days in an airtight container. Serve with beetroot hummus, sliced radish and fennel tops.

dinner.

BLACK PUMPKIN SALAD

Ingredients

Makes 2 mains or 5 starters
Time 40 minutes

DRESSING
2 garlic cloves, unpeeled
generous ½ cup (150 ml)
  orange juice
2 Tbsp extra virgin olive oil
sea salt and black pepper

SALAD
400 g (14 oz) pumpkin
2 garlic cloves, unpeeled
sea salt
2 Tbsp coconut oil
¾ cup (160 g) black rice
  or black rice noodles
3 Tbsp grated red
  cabbage
3 Tbsp thinly sliced apple
20 fresh mint leaves

Method

Preheat the oven to 180°C (350°F).

To make the dressing, roast the unpeeled garlic cloves for 20–25 minutes until cooked through. Let them cool, then remove the skin. Place all the ingredients for the dressing in a blender and mix to a creamy dressing.

Meanwhile, to make the salad, cut the pumpkin into equal large sections and place on a baking tray with the unpeeled garlic. Sprinkle with some sea salt and the coconut oil and bake in the oven for 20–30 minutes. Remove from the oven and let the pumpkin cool. Remove the seeds and cut into smaller slices.

Boil the black rice for about 30 minutes over low heat. Drain the rice and let it cool. If you are using black rice noodles, follow the instructions on the packet.

Put the rice or rice noodles in a bowl, then add the pumpkin, red cabbage and apple. Garnish with mint leaves and sprinkle with the dressing.

SWEET POTATO FRIES AND BEETROOT CROQUETTES WITH CASHEW MAYO

Ingredients

Makes 2 serves
Time 1 hour

CASHEW MAYO
¼ cup (40 g) cashew nuts
dash of lemon juice
fresh mint leaves

SWEET POTATO FRIES
1 large sweet potato
1 Tbsp sesame oil
1 tsp mixed spice

CROQUETTES
100 g (3½ oz) sweet
  potato, diced
100 g (3½ oz) beetroot,
  diced
1–2 garlic cloves
1½ handfuls of orange
  lentils
1 Tbsp grated ginger
1 x 190 g (7 oz) potato,
  unpeeled
dash of lemon juice
scant ½ cup (50 g)
  chickpea flour
1 Tbsp black sesame seeds
  (optional)
coconut oil, for frying

Method

To make the mayo, soak the cashew nuts for 30 minutes in boiling hot water and set aside.

To make the sweet potato fries, preheat the oven to 220°C (425°F). Cut the sweet potato lengthways into equal sections and rub with the oil and spice until well covered. Place the fries on a baking tray and bake for 20 minutes until cooked through, turning halfway through.

Meanwhile, start making the croquettes by boiling the sweet potato, beetroot, garlic, lentils and grated ginger for 45 minutes in a pan of boiling water.

Place the unpeeled potato in another pan with boiling water and boil for about 15–20 minutes until cooked through. Drain the water and let cool.

Drain the sweet potato mix too. Let it cool before you blend it to a creamy purée in a food processor. Place the purée in a large bowl and add the normal potato. Mash together roughly with a fork. Add some lemon juice and season the mixture with a pinch of sea salt. Use a teaspoon to make portions.

Roll the portions in the chickpea flour and black sesame seeds, if using, and shape them into long croquettes. Cook them in a frying pan in the hot coconut oil for a minute or two on each side until golden.

To finish the cashew mayo, drain the cashew nuts and put them in the food processor with 1–2 tablespoons of water or use a hand blender to make a creamy sauce. Season with some drops of lemon juice and the fresh mint leaves.

MELANZANA PASTA

Ingredients

Makes 2 serves
Time 1 hour

TAPENADE
**1 small eggplant
(aubergine)
2 large garlic cloves,
unpeeled
2 Tbsp extra virgin olive oil
pinch of sea salt**

**½ zucchini (courgette)
½ eggplant (aubergine)
1 or 2 halves of yellow
capsicum (pepper)
2 handfuls of pine nuts
150 g (5½ oz) wholegrain
pasta or noodles
extra virgin olive oil
grated zest of 1 lemon
15 fresh basil leaves**

Method

Preheat the oven to 180°C (350°F).

To make the tapenade, roast the unpeeled eggplant with the garlic cloves for 45 minutes until cooked through, taking out the garlic cloves after 25 minutes. Let everything cool and remove the skin from the eggplant and garlic. Using a blender or food processor, mix the eggplant and garlic with the olive oil and sea salt into a creamy tapenade.

Cut the zucchini and remaining eggplant into long thin slices and cut the capsicum in half. Grill all the pieces in a grill pan until light brown stripes appear, then flip everything and grill on the other side. Let the vegetables cool, cut the capsicum into equal-sized strips and then marinate all the vegetables in the tapenade.

Toast the pine nuts in a dry frying pan until golden.

Put the pasta or noodles in boiling hot water and cook following the instructions on the packet. Drain and add some olive oil and grated lemon zest. Put the pasta or noodles on 2 plates and divide the grilled vegetable mix between the plates. Sprinkle with the pine nuts and basil to serve.

MIDDLE-EASTERN STEW

Ingredients

Makes 2 serves
Time 1 hour

250 g (9 oz) baby carrots
3–4 Tbsp coconut oil
2 garlic cloves, unpeeled
1 tsp ras el hanout
  spice mix
350 g (12 oz) vitelotte
  purple potatoes,
  peeled and halved
1 bay leaf
5 black peppercorns
1 red onion, sliced
6 sprigs of fresh thyme
⅓ cup (75 ml) orange juice
sea salt and black pepper

GARNISH
1 handful of pistachio nuts,
  shelled and chopped
pinch of grated lemon zest

Method

Preheat the oven to 200°C (400°F).

Scrub the baby carrots and place them in an oven dish. Add 1 tablespoon of coconut oil and the garlic cloves.

Bake the carrots for 40 minutes, then sprinkle with the ras el hanout spice mix and cook for another 10 minutes.

While the carrots are baking, boil the potatoes with the bay leaf and peppercorns. Make sure that the potatoes are fully immersed and boil for 20 minutes over low heat. Turn off the heat and leave the potatoes to soak in the water for a few minutes.

Sauté the red onion in the remaining coconut oil and add half the thyme leaves at the end. Turn off the heat.

Take the carrots out of the oven and cut them into bite-sized pieces.

Peel the garlic cloves and mix together 1 clove, the remaining thyme and the orange juice to make a marinade. Sprinkle this over the carrot pieces and season with sea salt and black pepper. Let the carrots marinate while you make the purée.

Mash the potatoes with a hand blender or potato masher and add the second garlic clove. Season with sea salt and black pepper.

Serve the purée on the plates, add some marinated carrot and sprinkle the dish with chopped pistachio nuts, the red onion and thyme and the lemon zest.

TIP Purple potatoes not available? Choose parsnip or celeriac.

RAW CURRY WITH CHICKPEA AND CUMIN CRACKERS

Ingredients

Makes 2 serves
Time 10 minutes

SAUCE
50 g (2 oz) sunflower butter
  or white almond butter
1 tsp turmeric powder
1 tsp ground cumin
2/3 tsp ground cardamom
2/3 tsp ginger powder
1/2 tsp ground black pepper
1 garlic clove
dash of lemon juice
1/2 tsp sea salt

VEGETABLES
350 g (12 oz) rainbow carrots
2 handfuls of bean sprouts or
  pea shoots
2 handfuls of green peas,
  briefly cooked
2 handfuls of fresh coriander
  (cilantro) leaves

CRACKERS
1 cup (120 g) chickpea flour
1 Tbsp arrowroot powder
1 Tbsp cumin seeds
good pinch of sea salt
2 tsp coconut or sesame oil

Method

To make the sauce, use a hand blender to blend all the ingredients into a creamy mixture with 10 tablespoons hot water.

Cut the carrots lengthways into thin ribbons. Stir them into the sauce and leave to marinate.

To make the crackers, place the chickpea flour, arrowroot, cumin and salt in a bowl and stir together. Add the oil and 10 teaspoons of water drop by drop and knead into a sticky ball. Divide the ball into 4 portions.

Heat a frying pan over medium-high heat while you roll out the first ball into a cracker. The pan is ready when a drop of water sizzles right after you drop it in the pan. Make sure you have chickpea flour on your work surface, otherwise the pastry will stick. Take the first ball and roll it with your hands and a rolling pin until you have a thin disc or rectangle.

Place the cracker in the pan and wait 45–90 seconds until you see small bubbles appear and the colour change. Flip the cracker and cook for another 30–45 seconds. Remove it from the pan and repeat with the other crackers.

Add the bean sprouts, green peas and coriander to the carrot mix. Serve the curry sauce with the crackers.

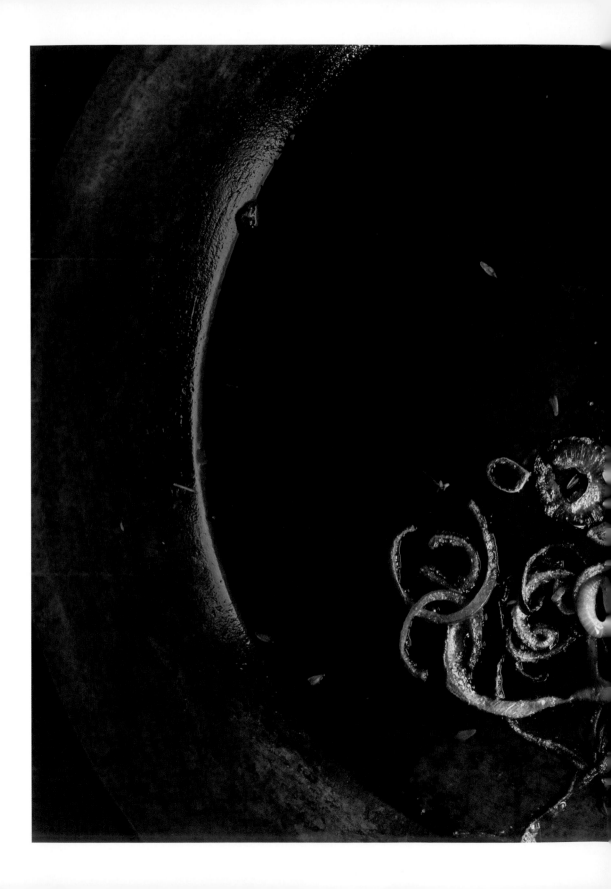

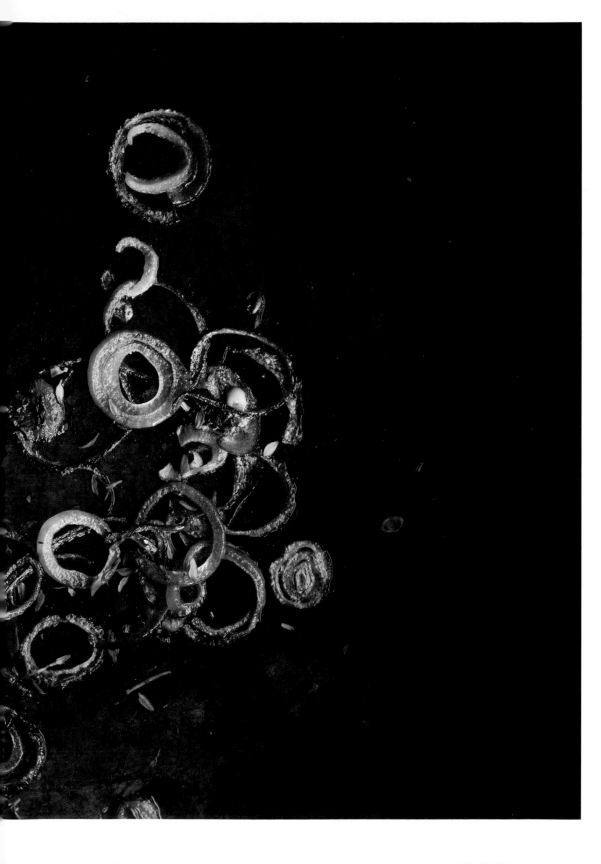

dessert.

COCONUT LAVENDER BONBONS

Ingredients

Makes about 12 bonbons
Time 5 minutes plus chilling

1 cup (60 g) shredded
   coconut
20 drops of vanilla extract
4 Tbsp rice syrup
4 Tbsp coconut oil
grated zest of 1 orange
1 full tsp lavender flowers

Method

Heat the coconut in a pan. Immediately add the vanilla, rice syrup, coconut oil, orange zest and flowers. Mix everything together well.

Turn off the heat and place the mixture in the freezer for 5 minutes.

Knead everything until firm. Shape into about 12 squares or rounds and put in the fridge for 15 minutes before serving.

dessert
gluten-free
autumn & winter

MELON SORBET WITH CRUNCH AND HERBS

Ingredients

Makes 2 serves
Time 2 minutes plus
  freezing

200 g (7 oz) melon
1 tsp pine nuts, chopped
**1 tsp pistachio nuts,
  chopped**
1 sprig of fresh basil

Method

Cut the melon into cubes and place them in the freezer overnight. Take them out of the freezer 10 minutes before you want to make the sorbet.

Thaw the cubes to room temperature and use a hand-held blender to make into a creamy sorbet. You may have to unplug the blender to remove the ice if it gets stuck. Mix it again after that and use an ice cream scoop to make into nice balls. Sprinkle with the pine nuts, chopped pistachio nuts and small leaves or flowers of the fresh basil.

TIP Make sure you always have fresh ripe seasonal fruit in the freezer. Then you can whip up a beautiful, simple and light dessert in no time.

dessert
gluten-free
autumn & winter

WALNUT AND PUMPKIN TARTS

Ingredients

Makes 3 x 5 cm (2 inch)
  tarts
Time 45 minutes plus
  freezing

TOPPING
1 Tbsp coconut oil
7 cardamom pods
5 cloves
150 g (5½ oz) pumpkin,
  cut into small cubes
2 Tbsp rice syrup

PASTRY
scant ½ cup (50 g) walnuts
sea salt
¾ cup (50 g) shredded
  coconut
2 Tbsp rice syrup
10 drops of vanilla extract
  or 1 vanilla bean

FILLING
3 large Tbsp coconut
  yoghurt or solids
  from top of a tin of
  coconut milk
1 large Tbsp rice syrup
10 drops of vanilla extract
  or 1 vanilla bean

Method

To make the topping, heat the oil in a pan. Add the cardamom and cloves and lightly fry everything. Add the pumpkin cubes after a few minutes. Stir so that all the pumpkin is covered in oil. Add the rice syrup. Let everything simmer for 30 minutes over very low heat until the rice syrup has almost evaporated. Meanwhile, make the pastry and the middle section.

To make the pastry, put the walnuts, a pinch of salt and the shredded coconut in a food processor. Turn it on and add the rice syrup little by little, then add the vanilla extract or the scrapings of the split vanilla bean. Turn the food processor off and knead the pastry with your hands. It is ready when you can shape it into a firm ball. Divide the pastry into 3 parts. Roll each part into a ball. Place each ball on the counter and press into a flat disc, then cut out a neat round with a 5 cm (2 inch) cutter. Place the 3 bases in the fridge.

To make the filling, combine the coconut yoghurt, rice syrup and vanilla extract or scrapings of the split vanilla bean with a spoon. Place this mixture in the fridge as well.

Now, take a thick piece of A4 paper. Put a dot every 9 cm (3½ inches) along the long edges. Cut on an imaginary line from dot to dot so you get 3 strips of 9 x 21 cm (3½ x 8 inches). Take the 3 bases out of the fridge and place the paper strips around the bases so they form a little tower – the diameter of the paper is 5 cm (2 inches) just like the base. Stick the paper strips together with tape. Spoon the coconut yoghurt evenly into the paper towers, over the bases. Place the tarts in the freezer for 30 minutes.

Spoon the cooled pumpkin topping into the 3 paper towers. Place in the freezer for as long as necessary to firm, then remove the paper strips, let them thaw a little and serve.

TIP You can make the tarts in advance and leave them frozen. Take them out of the freezer 20–30 minutes before serving.

dessert
gluten-free & raw
spring

MATCHA CREAM

Ingredients

Makes 2 serves
Time 5 minutes plus
   soaking

2 handfuls of cashew nuts
1 large banana
1 Tbsp matcha green tea
   powder

Method

Soak the cashew nuts overnight in enough water to cover them. Drain and rinse, then put them in a blender.

Add the banana and matcha powder along with a scant ½ cup (100 ml) of cold water and blend everything into a creamy mixture. Add your favourite seasonal topping to decorate and then serve.

MANGO CUSTARD

Ingredients

Makes 2–3 serves
Time 30 minutes plus
  chilling

40 g (1½ oz) dried mango
150 g (5½ oz) fresh mango
scant ½ cup (100 ml)
  coconut milk
juice of ½ lime
4 tsp arrowroot powder

OPTIONAL
4 Tbsp black sesame seeds
4 Tbsp coconut yoghurt

Method

Put the dried mango in a bowl and pour hot water over it to cover. Leave to soak for 7–10 minutes, then drain.

Place the dried mango, fresh mango, coconut milk, scant ½ cup (100 ml) of hot water and the lime juice in a blender and mix until creamy.

Mix the arrowroot with 4 teaspoons of cold water and set aside.

Put the mango cream in a pan and heat over low heat until you see steam rise. Do not let it boil! Mix the arrowroot paste with the mango cream and heat it for 2–4 minutes over low heat until the cream becomes firm. Turn off the heat and pour the cream into 2 glasses. Put them in the fridge for 30 minutes.

Toast the sesame seeds in a dry frying pan. Garnish the custards with coconut yoghurt and the sesame seeds and serve.

TIP No fresh mango? You can also use frozen mango pieces. The lime can also be replaced with lemon.

GRACELAND ICE CREAM CAKE

Ingredients

Makes 1 x 16 cm (6 inch) cake
Time 50 minutes plus freezing

BASE
⅓ cup (45 g) unsalted peanuts
⅔ cup (45 g) shredded coconut
¼ cup (45 g) Medjool dates, pitted and diced
sea salt

FILLING
1 large ripe banana
50 g (2 oz) pure peanut butter
a few drops of lime or lemon juice

TOPPING
1 coconut
½ Tbsp coconut milk
1 Tbsp rice syrup
1 Tbsp coconut oil
1 tsp lime or lemon juice
edible flowers or fruit

Method

To make the base, place the peanuts, shredded coconut and diced dates in a food processor or use a hand-held blender to mix everything up. Press this 'pastry' firmly into a 16 cm (6 inch) cake tin. Sprinkle with a pinch of sea salt and put the cake tin in the fridge for 30 minutes. Now start making the filling and topping.

To make the filling, use a blender to combine all the ingredients into a creamy mixture. Cover and place in the fridge.

To make the topping, open the coconut, remove the brown parts and cut the white parts into small pieces – you need 50 g (2 oz) coconut flesh. Put the coconut flesh, coconut milk, syrup, oil and juice in a food processor or use a hand-held blender to combine it into a creamy topping. Let it run for at least 5 minutes and stir around occasionally. The longer you let it run, the creamier and lighter the topping will be.

Pour the filling over the cake base. Place in the freezer for 30 minutes, then pour the topping over the filling and place in the freezer for another 90 minutes.

Decorate with edible flowers or fruit. Cut the cake and let it thaw for 5–10 minutes before taking your first bite.

TIP Never opened a coconut? It is very easy (and YouTube has several videos on this). Save the remainder of the coconut flesh in a sealable container in the fridge and use it as a snack or in curries or desserts. Is there coconut water in the nut? Drink it! There is nothing better than coconut water. Don't feel like trying? Then use the solid parts from a tin of coconut milk instead of a whole coconut.

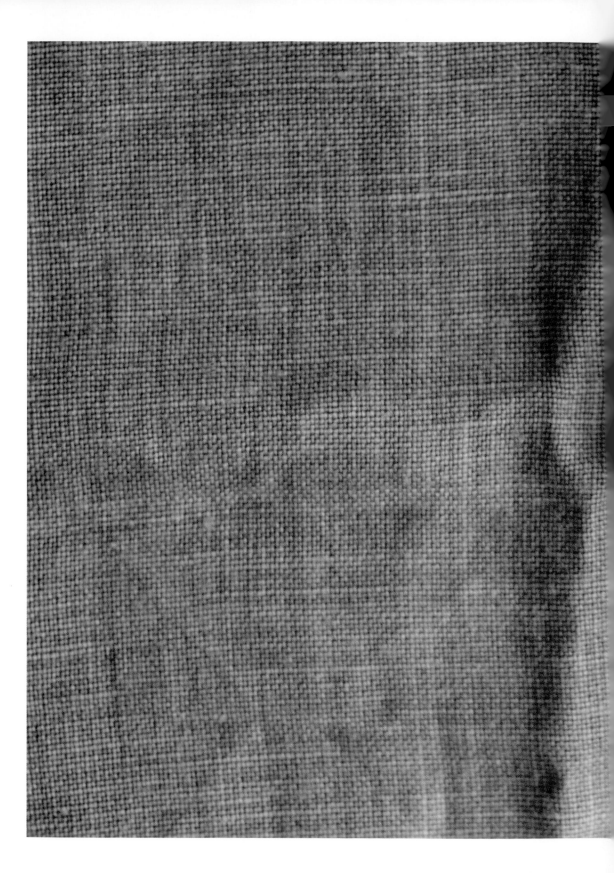